Garter Snakes

A Pet Care Guide for Garter Snakes

Garter Snakes General Info, Purchasing, Care, Cost, Keeping, Health, Supplies, Food, Breeding and More Included!

By Lolly Brown

Copyrights and Trademarks

All rights reserved. No part of this book may be reproduced or transformed in any form or by any means, graphic, electronic, or mechanical, including photocopying, recording, taping, or by any information storage retrieval system, without the written permission of the author.

This publication is Copyright ©2017 NRB Publishing, an imprint. Nevada. All products, graphics, publications, software and services mentioned and recommended in this publication are protected by trademarks. In such instance, all trademarks & copyright belong to the respective owners. For information consult www.NRBpublishing.com

Disclaimer and Legal Notice

This product is not legal, medical, or accounting advice and should not be interpreted in that manner. You need to do your own due-diligence to determine if the content of this product is right for you. While every attempt has been made to verify the information shared in this publication, neither the author, neither publisher, nor the affiliates assume any responsibility for errors, omissions or contrary interpretation of the subject matter herein. Any perceived slights to any specific person(s) or organization(s) are purely unintentional.

We have no control over the nature, content and availability of the web sites listed in this book. The inclusion of any web site links does not necessarily imply a recommendation or endorse the views expressed within them. We take no responsibility for, and will not be liable for, the websites being temporarily unavailable or being removed from the internet.

The accuracy and completeness of information provided herein and opinions stated herein are not guaranteed or warranted to produce any particular results, and the advice and strategies, contained herein may not be suitable for every individual. Neither the author nor the publisher shall be liable for any loss incurred as a consequence of the use and application, directly or indirectly, of any information presented in this work. This publication is designed to provide information in regard to the subject matter covered.

Neither the author nor the publisher assume any responsibility for any errors or omissions, nor do they represent or warrant that the ideas, information, actions, plans, suggestions contained in this book is in all cases accurate. It is the reader's responsibility to find advice before putting anything written in this book into practice. The information in this book is not intended to serve as legal, medical, or accounting advice.

Foreword

Found in various locations of the United States and with most widely available in the breeding and pet trade, the garter snake, in its many varieties are readily available for would be owners. The beauty about garter snakes is their active daytime lifestyle making them perfect viewing pets that are animatedly active during the day, compared to other reptiles that are typically asleep during the day and awake at night.

Discover the fascinating characteristics of the garter snake and get to know more about their traits which are alluring, mysterious, curious, unique and absolutely fascinating. Have a look at where you can get anyone of these colorfully wonderful reptiles to take in as pets and what it would take for you to get one or even a couple.

Table of Contents

Introduction 1

Chapter One: Biological Information 3

    Classification, Origin and Distribution 4

    The Subspecies of Garter Snakes 6

    Size, Life Span, and Physical Appearance 10

    Garter Snake Trivias 12

Chapter Two: Garter Snakes as Pets 15

    What Makes It a Great Pet 16

    Pros and Cons of Garter Snakes 17

    Snake Licensing 18

    Cost of Owning a Snake 19

Chapter Three: Purchasing and Selecting a Healthy Breed . 21

    Where to Purchase a Garter Snake Breed 22

    How to Spot a Good Garter Snake Breeder 24

    Characteristics of a Healthy Breed 26

Chapter Four: Habitat Requirements for Garter Snakes 27

    How to Set Up Your Snake's Enclosure 28

    Regulating Temperature 31

Chapter Five: Nutrition and Feeding 33

    Nutritional Needs of Garter Snakes 34

Feeding Conditions and How to Feed Your Garter Snakes..36

Feeding Amount and Frequency 37

Chapter Six: Maintenance for Garter Snakes......................... 39

Spot Cleaning Your Snake's Enclosure................................ 40

Husbandry Tips and Guidelines on How to Clean Your Snake's Enclosure... 42

Illnesses caused by Unsanitary and Unhealthy Living Conditions 44

Chapter Seven: Dealing and Handling Your Garter Snakes 47

Dealing With and Taming Your Garter Snake 49

Taming Your Garter Snake... 50

Chapter Eight: Breeding Your Garter Snakes......................... 55

Sexual Dimorphism and Behavior....................................... 56

How to Set Up the Right Breeding Conditions 57

Successful Garter Snake Breeding....................................... 59

The Birthing of Garters 60

Caring for Newborn and Juvenile Garter Snakes............ 62

Life Cycle of a Garter Snake... 64

Chapter Nine: Common Diseases and Treatments for Garter Snakes... 67

Common Minor Problems.. 68

Common Major Problems 72

> **Other Health Issues** **74**

Chapter Ten: Garter Snake Summary 77

> **What Makes It a Great Pet** **81**
>
> **Maintenance for Garter Snakes** **84**
>
> **Glossary of Snake Terms** **89**

Index 97

Photo Credits 103

References 105

Introduction

Welcome to the wonderful world of herpetology! Our focus in this book is the truly diverse species of garter snakes, with an impressive 35 specie variation each with their own individual variety of colors and sizes that would fit the desires of anyone looking into taking in any one of these beautiful creatures.

You will get to know each of them and which ones can be kept as pets and ones that you will need special permits for and why. You will find out about what they eat, how to house them as well as their requirements. Learn how

Introduction

to breed them, or at the very least what to expect should you not be sure about the sex of the ones you have.

Even when seen in the wild, a garter snake, if picked up will usually be agreeable to handling and not attack, as long as handled with a mild approach. It would usually just coil up on itself, on your hand and would sit there, just as curious as about you as you are of it. If it does get spooked it emanates an odor from its coacal to ward off offensive handling. The garter snake would usually use this tactic to ward off would be predators.

There are many breeders of this beautiful species of various sorts so wild ones are hardly ever (and rightfully should be left alone in the wilderness) sold in the pet trade. Getting in touch with a thoughtful breeder will be another one of the important topics we shall be discussing in this book.

Chapter One: Biological Information

Many people make the mistake of getting a pet without looking into what entails caring for one. Going headlong into acquiring a pet would be a really irresponsible thing to do because a pet, once taken in depends on the owner for all of its needs and requirements to live a happy, healthy and long life.

Caring for reptiles is a lot more tricky than one would expect because as much as we wouldn't want to call it high maintenance, it does require a certain level of attention and care that isn't as simple as setting out food for it or making sure it does not escape. And this is what we aim to reveal to you with our compilation of information about the garter snake. Find out all about the different sorts of garter snakes available for you to choose from and get the low down on what it would take for you to take in and care for them.

Classification, Origin and Distribution

Garter snakes come from the subfamily of colubridae snakes and are found within the main lands of America. Typically sporting patterns of yellow stripes on their bodies of either color green, brown or black backgrounds, it is now more common to see other columbrids with different morph coloration in the pet trade.

They range in length depending on their specie but the most common ones are about 22 to 54 inches and weigh an average of about 5.5 ounces. When left to exist in nature, these tiny little guys who are often found clustered together more than they are independently, live up to about 5 years. That length of longevity extends doubly when bred and raised in captivity.

They are found in many regions, areas and states across the United States of America. They're found in New Mexico, Oregon, and Mississippi. Others are found in many parts of California. There are others that call Chicago their home. You will also find many garter snakes in Texas.

Chapter One: Biological Information

A number of them are indigenous to areas like the Hernando County in Florida. There are also those found in the eastern part of the Florida Gulf coast. Others call the coastal area of the Pacific Northwest, namely Washington, their home. Garter snakes have also been imported overseas, like Sweden and Canada.

There are garter snake species that are found along the eastern Mississippi shores and then there are others that are diversely widespread across New England. As much as garter snakes live and inhabit a variety of locations and ecosystems, which we shall discuss in more detail as we go along, one thing is common amongst most of them; they prefer to live in areas that are close to any sort of body of water making them hunters and predators of most amphibians.

They can frequently be found in urban areas as well! And these are not the sort your reptile-loving neighbor has next door and took in as pet; they have been spotted in places where people are present but where they are still mostly hidden from plain sight, like parks, sewers or ditches, old fallen logs, stone walls, forests, bogs, swampy marshlands, hillsides and the likes - again, not too far from where there is some sort of body of water present.

Chapter One: Biological Information

There are over a dozen species and subspecies of garter snakes spread out all across the United States and North America. Most garter snake species and subspecies have reached other shores and have been introduced to different countries, hence their popularity amongst herpetologists and reptile aficionados have become widely popular the world over.

The Subspecies of Garter Snakes

Out in the wild, these columbrides live up to 4-5 years given the conditions of being exposed not only to the elements, they also have to contend with others for food not only with their own sort but also with other animals they share ecosystems and habitat. A very different picture is painted when they are in captivity, exponentially increasing their chances of survival and there have been many garter snake enthusiasts who have reported their garter snakes to live up to 10 years or so. Let's get to know some of them and find out more about these fascinating reptiles as we read about them in this chapter of this book.

Eastern Garter Snake

The eastern garter snake averages a length of about 18-24 inches with females out-lengthening males. Aside from their striped pattern the eastern garter snakes come in many

Chapter One: Biological Information

various colors such as black, brown and green with distinctly contrasting body stripe markings along the length of its body in either white or yellow.

Red-Spotted Garter Snakes

These garter snakes call the marshes, damp lands of Western Oregon. They are also found in the coastal towns of California and SD County Valley.

San Fransisco Garter Snake

The thamnophis sirtalis tetrataenia is a native of central western part of California, particularly in the San Mateo County in the brackish estuaries of San Francisco.

Santa Cruz Garter Snake

Found in the ranges of California and Oregon, the Thamnophis atratus atratus is a subspecies that amazingly colour morphs from a sole line of strip to 3 strips which run down its back.

Bluestripe Garter Snakes

Bluestripe garter snakes get their moniker from the blue stripes which are found on their spine as well as dorsal scales just above the stomach of their graceful bodies. These snakes also have their own unique look given their light brownish flecks on each side and set in the middle of their ridged dorsal scales. The blue stripe garter snake is protected garter snake specie and is illegal to own as a pet or have in captivity unless the individual who has one has a permit to have one.

The Mexican Garter Snake

The Mexican Garter Snake used to slither aplenty in numbers in the Arizona, but now only a few groups of these beautiful slip, slider, crawlers are isolated in the south central region of the state as well as the rim beneath it which is why it is currently a protected species in Arizona with mandates to leave it be and not make any sort of contact with it.

Valley Garter Snake

Can be found in the many basins of California and their range is wide from Siskiyou county, Sacramento county, the foothills of Sierra Nevada, North Humboldt county, and so many other regions of this particular area of the United States. Various species with varied patterns and colors - all sharing the same one strip on the back and two flanking each side of the snake - are prevalent in these parts of California.

California Red – sided Garter Snake

California red-sided garter snake is one of the more if not the most colorful of all garter snakes. With fiery flecks of red patterns over its predominantly black body with usually white sometimes blue stripe markings running the length of its back and either side of the snake this elegantly beautiful beast is an impressive sight to behold, more so when you notice its sometimes blue hued undercarriage. It occurs in a wide range of the basins and valleys as well as the marsh and wet lands of California. The red-sided garter snakes have relatively bigger eyes than other garter snakes and averages 38 inches.

It is one of the better swimmers amongst the garter snake species and dines on a variety of food like small frogs, lizards, the occasional bird, an unlucky mouse in the wild. It is like most other garter snakes tolerant and immune to newt toxins.

Puget Sound Garter Snake

This red flecked sided snake native of the regions of Washington grows up to a meter long. The Puget Sound Garter Snake is said to be easier to identify because of the difference of female and male tails; with the male Puget SGS snake's tail thicker and longer at the base. Whilst other snakes have no tolerance for newts, this native of Washington has developed a tolerance for them whilst others have not.

Size, Life Span, and Physical Appearance

The garter snake is perhaps one of the most popular choices for reptile lovers not only for its relative calm disposition but also for their grace aneroid variety in colors and lengths. Join me as we take a closer look at each of these amazingly gorgeous creations of nature.

- Eastern Garter Snake: It is named such because of its strap - like appearance. The Eastern Garter Snake is a New Latin term because of its striped pattern look. The California Garter Snakes amazingly morph in two distinct colors of three stripes along its graceful body, typical of garter snakes; and another with a lone stripe which runs down its lengthy 18-55 inch back.

- San Francisco Garter Snake: This beautifully colorful garter snake species, known as the San Francisco garter snake, is protected and has sadly been listed as endangered by the law since 1969, citing the

Chapter One: Biological Information

predation of crayfish for their decline in numbers. This means that it is illegal to keep or purvey them unless the individual with intent to do so is or has been allowed by governing authorities and agencies to do so.

- The Red-Spotted Garter Snake: This subspecies of the garter snake is a compelling vision with its deep ebony base scales, and a red spotted cranium. It measures in at 18-52 inches and is one of the more common ones of its kind.

- Bluestripe Garter Snake: Another subspecies of the garter snake is the Bluestripe. This garter snake matures to an average length of about 26 inches. The maximum length of a bluestripe garter snake was recorded to be close to 40 inches!

- The Mexican Garter Snake: Measuring in at 44 inches, they come in olive-brown color, others red-brown garter snake with a creamy stripe trailing it back is vivid with thin dark lines flanking the cream strip of distinction.

Chapter One: Biological Information

Garter Snake Trivias

- Male common garter snakes would have a field day and will vie and attempt to breed with one femalem after brumation and during breeding season. They can be quite a sight to see in the wild!

- Common garter snakes give birth to live snakes, unlike other snakes that usually lay their eggs. Common garter snakes have evolved to become resistant to tetrodotoxin, a poisonous substance found in ocean sunfish, puffer fish, porcupine fish and aquatic newts, so much so that they are able to absorb this toxin into their system making them poisonous to potential predators.

- The downside to this immunity to this neuro - toxin though is that it makes them temporarily immobilized and lethargic for a considerable length of time.

- Baby or young garter snakes at birth can average a length of about 9 inches long at the most and 5 inches long at the least. They are incubated inside of the mother, hatching out of their shells inside of the gravid female.

Chapter One: Biological Information

- Most garter snakes species have dual-colored tongues. They also come in various colors and patterns depending on their sort. The reports of species and subspecies of garter snakes morphing to various bright colors apart from the usual striped patterns down their backs have made them even more fascinating creatures.

- They shed a number of times each year with their initial shed happening right after they emerge from their mother.

- These snakes are one of the most studied and recorded amongst others because of the evolution of their changes and morph phases. One example of this would be the recently observed flame morph which have been making more of an appearance in some garter snake species and are available in the reptile trade.

- The maximum measured length of a garter snake can reach up to 5 feet. Most of them have a strip of contrasting color which runs down their backs and two more flanking each side of the snake.

Chapter One: Biological Information

Chapter Two: Garter Snakes as Pets

It may or may not come as a surprise to many of you that there have been many garter snakes aficionados whose interest in these generally docile snakes started early because they are diurnal snakes they are most active during the daytime therefore are easily spotted when out in the wild. This is a great trait for those who are early risers and daytime people because it allows them to enjoy watching, socializing and handling their garter snakes during daylight hours. Whereas many other snake species are most active at night, garter snakes are often up and about whilst the sun is up.

Grown men and women today have been known to have started their love for the garter snake since they were wee ones, out playing with their friends in the fields and near waterways. Discovering the beauty and elegance of these tiny little guys and seeing their graceful demeanor, they are enraptured. Since this species is relatively unaggressive and although they do possess a certain amount of venom, theirs is the kind which is not toxic to humans but would cause considerable damage to their prey.

This chapter aims to highlight the characteristics, traits and behaviors of garter snakes with an attempt to explain what it is that compels us to take them in and why they make excellent pets for novice and experienced herps.

What Makes It a Great Pet

These attractive, considerably small and generally docile snakes are easy to be around and make for hours and hours of viewing them a pleasure. They are not aggressive and are usually accepting of frequent handling by their owners. Garter snakes get along relatively well with other snakes when housed together with those who are not snake-eaters. Be sure to research your existing pet snake to make sure that it does not prey on smaller snakes, because there are species of snakes that do eat other slithers. You wouldn't want that at all. When housed together with their sort and kind you will find them actively social with each other. They like to huddle together during cold winter months and

Chapter Two: Garter Snakes as Pets

"steal" warmth from each other and keep each other company. As long as they are kept with same sized snakes that won't make attempts to gobble them up, they are cool being with other snakes. Given that the traits of the other snake specie are peaceful and agreeable to having other snake specie for company.

Pros and Cons of Garter Snakes

It is kind of difficult to mention downsides to owning a garter snake because there is very little fault to find with them. Apart from the usual stuff like special lighting, heating, temperature and humidity control, garter snakes are a joy to watch and care for. As mentioned earlier they are pretty mild mannered and would just be happy to be in a terrarium or vivarium that would mimic their natural habitat. Their saliva does have properties toxic to their prey but are harmless to humans. A small number of individuals who have been bit by garter snakes, at the very worst would experience a rash which goes away on its own soon enough.

A downside we can think of is being surprised by the number of live snakes a gravid female can give birth to if an owner is not knowledgeable of the gravid and birthing process of garter snakes. Be sure to get ready for more rather than less and set your expectations high in order to be ready for the unexpected when caring for a heavily gravid female or two.

Snake Licensing

If you own a San Francisco garter snake then you must have a permit to do so. If you are lucky enough to have obtained a license and are now keeping one, you should know that it thrives in a 60 percent humidity range, needs to be housed in an enclosure with temps ranging from 75 to 85 degrees F. This native of the outback of San Francisco would also need to be housed in an enclosure with a heating pad (ideally located under its tank) with temps ranging between 90 to 95 degrees. Most garter snakes are common in the United States save for the one we just discussed needing a special permit to own. Otherwise garter snakes of many species and subspecies are readily available in the reptile trade and are fairly cheap to acquire.

The Western terrestrial garter snake as well as the Plains garter snake is also two other exceptions that would need you to secure a permit for depending on the number you wish to own and keep. These two subspecies of the garter snake may be owned provided that no more than a dozen is owned by one individual.

Chapter Two: Garter Snakes as Pets

Cost of Owning a Snake

Garter snakes are born live and the litter can be anywhere from 4 to 42 snakelets, this can be a large average margin but is also a reality. And should you start considering breeding them, then you will have to have deep pockets and good solid plan at the very onset of taking in pairs that would and could breed.

The availability of garter snakes in the pet trade is aplenty and available readily. So the simple acquisition of one will not make too much of a dent on your wallet. It is the long term raising, maintain, and feeding for which you want to be prepare.

Depending on the simplicity or the intricacy of housing you decide to provide your garner snakes will be a big factor on your finances. Many garter snake owners have experimented over the years on the easiest and most cost effective methods of housing and feeding because these will come hand in hand as you will later read. Again, depending on the number of garter snakes you have or decide to take in will also determine how many enclosures you will need to purchase, outfit with heating mats, thermal regulators, substrate and proper lighting. All these equate to initial purchases, i.e. machines that would heat and regulate the temperatures in the enclosures. These spell a monthly increase in your energy costs.

Food will not come cheap especially if you have a lot of these little monsters in your care. As you get to know your garter snakes so will you get to know their appetites; in the wild they feed on fish, tadpoles, and frogs. The diet expands a little more when garter snakes are raised in captivity. Garter snakes raised by loving humans at home feed on mice, pinkies, live fish, meal worms and earthworms. So the truth of the matter is depending on how many you keep is how you will be spending. We came up with a small chart below showing the cost of one garter snake upon acquisition, as well as the weekly, monthly and annual financial dent.

Chapter Three: Purchasing and Selecting a Healthy Breed

No one wants to get a sick pet, unless it is their intention of nursing one back to health. This route takes a big heart, a lot of patience and a deep pocket of cash. So unless this is your intention, read on to learn how spot a healthy and unwell garter snake. It doesn't take too much to spot traits of illness or wellness if the potential owner does the necessary research. We aim to shed light and give you the low down on what to look out for so you know what you are getting. You being here show that you are doing the responsible thing by finding out what you need to know.

Chapter Three: Purchasing and Selecting a Healthy Breed

Don't be one of the many of those who have made previous mistakes of not doing the proper research and ended up with a broken heart. The thing about reptiles is that they are wired to not show illness. This is a defense mechanism employed by reptiles in the wild in order to avoid being prey to predator. So, not catching the signs or recognizing red flags may result to a gravely ill pet. Shall we delve deeper into this topic? Let's do that now.

Where to Purchase a Garter Snake Breed

You would think that a pet store would be the ideal place to get a garter snake since they are conspicuously out in the open and apparently have been given license to sell. But think twice. As much as many of the employees who face everyday customers love animals and being around them, they aren't always given the proper information about how the animals got there, what conditions they were in during transport, or if they were bred by conscientious breeders or caught in the wild. It is a possibility that they will not be in any position to give you any sort of health guarantees either.

The internet seems to be one of the most obvious places to look for a garter snake and sure, there are reputable ones who advertise online and people who have purchased without hitches or hiccups, but buyers beware as there are

Chapter Three: Purchasing and Selecting a Healthy Breed

more out there on the Internet who are simply out to make a quick buck and separate you and your cash without thought or consideration. Go ahead and check out the Internet, but it will be a gamble to just randomly click and deal with the first one who responds IF you don't know what to look for then your hopes of a having a happy pet garter snake could end up with an unhappy ending. You want to be able to identify if the breeder is concerned about the future of the garter snake so make sure that you are doing the right thing by getting the proper feedback and reviews of the breeder you are planning to do business with.

Our best advice is to network with equally thoughtful herpetologists and snake owners to ask for their input, especially those who have been successful in raising their own healthy ones. Another good source of information is your herp vet, which you want to locate very early on, even before making a purchase. A reptile vet specialist is not only rare, but being rare are they are, they would be able to point out people who have been recently successful in breeding snakes. Yes, your best bets are to ask those who have recently been successful in breeding healthy garter snakes. We wish you all the best in finding one and allow us to go an extra mile by doing you a solid as we let you in on what to look out for when dealing with breeders of garter snakes; to sift out the unscrupulous from the upstanding ones.

Chapter Three: Purchasing and Selecting a Healthy Breed

How to Spot a Good Garter Snake Breeder

First you will have to study up on the garter snake sort you wish to acquire. This not only gives you an overview of what you need to look out for, it will also help narrow down your options and let you make an intelligent decision about which garter snake specie you want to take home with you.

You want to run, and run away fast, from breeders who are only concerned about your credit card going through online. You can't trust a breeder who won't allow you a visit to their facilities in order for you to check out the conditions their animals live in. If they do allow this, then make sure that you know what you are looking out for and that you are able to identify the signs that may or may not give indication of how the animals are treated.

You don't want to deal with breeders who can't answer basic questions like what sort of breeding methods were employed. You can't trust anyone who can't give you straight answers about the health of the lot of snakes. Nor can you take the word of someone who gives flowery, agreeable answers. This goes for those who give you dodgy answers to simple questions about what the snakes have been feeding on. And you most certainly don't want to deal

Chapter Three: Purchasing and Selecting a Healthy Breed

with anyone who cannot give you any sort of health guarantee.

A good breeder will be ready to give you honest answers and not empty promises. They would be able to upfront about their methods of breeding, how long they have been doing it, they would be happy to tell you of their failures and ultimate success. They wouldn't have any qualms about sharing their failures and heartbreaks which ultimately taught them to be better and more effective breeders.

Breeders who have been traversing a constant path of learning would be able to give you sound advice about how to take care of a garter snake with confidence. They would be ready to receive and welcome you to their facilities so that you can check out the living conditions of the animals for yourself.

Good breeders would even be happy to have you take home stuff that the snake has been using like their enclosure, vitamins and whatnots. Good breeders would also be in the know about the gender of the snakes taking great care in the process of identification - this is not an easy procedure and could harm, hurt and injure the snake if done incorrectly.

Chapter Three: Purchasing and Selecting a Healthy Breed

Characteristics of a Healthy Breed

Compared to other columbrides, garter snakes are considered small in length measuring in at a minimum ranging from 23 to 30 inches and at a maximum of 5 feet. Acquiring a garter snake of healthy stock is important not only so that you raise a happy garter snake, but it is more so vital if you later expect to breed your garter snakes. Garter snakes are naturally active in the wild and can be seen moving about frequently in nature. This holds true too for those bred in captivity and even more so because of interaction and socialization. A sluggish garter snake is never a good sign of health.

Be sure to inspect the garter snakes skin, especially if acquiring or adopting an adult garter snake, and check for skin blisters or lumps which may signal parasitic infestation. Check that the scales of the garter snake is not flaking (apart from the natural skin shedding) because this could be a sign of an ill snake. If the garter snake is amenable to be picked up and you hear breathing difficulties in the form of panting or wheezing, then it most likely has a cold or it could be the onset of pneumonia which can be passed on from one reptile to another. Salmonella is a problem that is present in most reptiles so be sure to wash your hands before and after handling a garter snake.

Chapter Four: Habitat Requirements for Garter Snakes

The joys of being able to watch your garter snakes in action in a terrarium set up to mimic its natural habitat is not only a joy to look at but it also gives your garter snakes the experience of living in its own ecosystem consistent, or as closely as it can be, to how it would live out in the wild. Of course it cannot exactly be completely comparable if it were living in nature as you have basically given them a greater chance by being cared for different conditions. Because of your watchful and mindful care, they are no longer in peril of from sudden death by predator.

Chapter Four: Habitat Requirements for Garter Snakes

Would be garter snake eaters are now out of the picture since you are going to be largely responsible for its nourishment. Having the luxury of living in an environment you set up for them, rids them of what would have been a daily task of hunting and foraging for food and sets them up for consistency as long as you follow the living, heating, humidity, and ecological necessities they would need to thrive and thrive well.

How to Set Up Your Snake's Enclosure

Garter snakes are considered to be generalists, living in places such as meadows, near marsh and swampy lands. They are often found huddled in groups burrowed beneath the earth in forest woodlands where they have easy access to bask for warmth when the sun is out.

Many of them are excellent swimmers, and can hand around waterways which thrive with food they like. Garter snakes like to live in areas near the water where tiny fish, newts, grogs, worms, earthworms and other small mammals are present to provide them prey and food.

In captivity, you would ideally want to house your juvenile garter pets in 16 ounce jars or enclosures for a few weeks in order for you to be able to observe them

Chapter Four: Habitat Requirements for Garter Snakes

individually. This practice of separating them from a larger population for a week or two gives you the advantage of getting to know each one of them. It allows you to be able to identify their individual markings, traits, characteristics, like, dislikes and behavior. It also makes for easier socialization. It is also a fuss-free method of feeding them.

A thirty gallon tank would be the ideal size tank to house a pair of breeding garter snakes. Naturally you would want a larger sized terrarium for a bigger bunch of these relatively smaller than most slithers to occupy a larger more comfortable space. Be sure that the tank is covered properly and securely with a double mesh net because these little monsters are excellent escapists. As long as their heads manage to push through an opening then the rest of their body can slither just as easily through it. Once you determine the number of snakes you would like to house together and decide on the size of their space enclosure, it is then that you want to figure out what you need and how you should be out fitting the enclosure.

There are those who keep their garter snakes in a series of enclosed and shady racks - much like little drawers, but these little critters are such a joy to look at that it would be such a shame to keep them hidden away.

Chapter Four: Habitat Requirements for Garter Snakes

This is when networking with other experienced garter snake owner/keepers comes in handy. Many experienced reptile keepers have been keen on making their snake's habitat suitable and appropriate for their needs, and you being here, reading with interest on this species, should be just as concerned about providing them the needful.

You can choose from mesh-like enclosures or acrylic ones. If you have the money to spend then opt for a glass aquarium. Start out by disinfecting the tank making sure that once you are ready to lay down bedding the vivarium is prepared for a fresh bed of the right substrate. Lay out the enclosure with sufficiently sized pieces of branches they can traverse, a hollowed out log or two where your snakes can camp out, some vine or aquatic plants where they can climb up and down on, and set out a few places where your garter snake can hide.

Check out samples on the internet. Be creative and make sure that you check out the proper sort of plants and substrate you can use. All these are for the benefit of your garter snakes and them getting the proper amount of exercise as well as giving you the opportunity to enjoy them play, frolic, relax, interact with each other, and just be what they are - fascinating creatures to behold.

Chapter Four: Habitat Requirements for Garter Snakes

Regulating Temperature

Reptiles are cold-blooded creatures unable to produce heat on their own and need the assistance of nature when they are in the wild to be able to heat their bodies. Keep in mind that in the wild, garter snakes take the opportunity to sit out under the sun to bask to absorb heat. The temperature inside of the habitat you would have fashioned for the garter snakes should have a gradient temperature of about 74 - 82 degrees Fahrenheit.

In captivity, you as its keeper will need to provide it with the proper basking spaces with temperatures ranging between 90 - 95 degrees. You would be glad to know that keeping them in temperature controlled spaces not only allows them to get the much needed heat they require, this also allows them to digest their food better. Use a heating lamp firmly affixed to one side of the tank or uses a heating pad.

UV light is a great source of lighting that can make up for the lack of natural light which allows them produce calcium naturally. It may not be absolutely necessary to set up a UV light system but it is advisable. If absolutely unable, make sure that you supplement them with much needed

Chapter Four: Habitat Requirements for Garter Snakes

calcium through powder form which you can mix in with their food when it is feeding time.

Humidity levels can be assisted with the mix of a shallow water dish half-filled with water. This makes for a good place to cool down its body, clean itself and drink. Make sure that there are no contaminants in the water dish by providing it a fresh bowl regularly or as needed - because you never know when the water can get spoilt by a piece of regurgitated food or snake vomitus.

Chapter Five: Nutrition and Feeding

Aside from the proper enclosure cleanliness and requirements of a reptile, food is a source of life and nourishment your garter snake's health will hinge on and you will have to know what to provide for it and what your garter snake would need. Make sure that you factor in the expense and effort it will take for you to choose only the best for your slithering buddy because doing so will only optimize its growth and balance. Not minding what you feed your garter snake will pave way for its health to deteriorate and give way for its immune system to weaken.

We compiled information to give you better confidence and so you know what your garter snake will need in order for the both of you to enjoy each other's company for a long time to come. Read on to find out what the basic nutritional needs of your snake will need and where to get it. You will also find out how to feed it properly without harming it or yourself. Come step into this lair.

Nutritional Needs of Garter Snakes

Garter snakes in the wild get the majority of their food around locations where there is water where there is an abundance of food sources they prey upon. Typical garter snakes have evolved to develop immunity to poisonous rough-skinned newts. Whilst other snakes who may attempt to eat them could successfully get them in their mouths and systems, the poisonous newt toxins, called tetrodotoxin, would eventually get them in the end.

Garter snakes have developed a tolerance for newts at a level where the garter snake is actually able to absorb the toxin of the newt into their system which wards off would be predators. This is an advantage to them because this makes them unsavory to their own predators. Most garter snakes prefer to stick near water ways to hunt for earthworms, voles, fish, newts and the occasional small mammal that may unsuspectingly cross a garter snakes path.

Chapter Five: Nutrition and Feeding

Garter snakes in the wild would thrive on newts, small amphibians and mammals, fish, night crawlers, meal worms, slug to name a few. When in the care of a herp keeper it is important for the potential caregiver to introduce foods like pinkies as this will actually be readily more available and cheaper than fish. You don't want to raise choosy garter snakes therefore be patient when introducing foods.

Garter snakes are not big fans of insects so let's just get that out there and out of the way so you need not have to learn the hard way. Red wigglers are worms which produce a smelly, sticky, bitter orangey - yellowish slime that could most likely make your garter snake very, very ill which could actually cause it to die. So be careful not to feed them these red wigglers marketed under names like trout worms, compost worms or Pan fish. As much as possible feed them fresh food that has been recently cut up, i.e. earthworms, meal worms, night crawlers which bait shops carry. If you are harvesting them yourself, then make sure that you are not collecting them from places where you know pesticides have been used.

Chapter Five: Nutrition and Feeding

Feeding Conditions and How to Feed Your Garter Snakes

Remember when talked about how housing, enclosures habitat and feeding taking up a chunk of not only money, your careful efforts and time? Well let's discuss this more for a bit now. Raising a number of garter snakes all at once will see you going through hits and misses on this one and we wish you all the good fortune and wisdom from the get go so you get to raise them all well.

Do not attempt to place food randomly or just drop them into the enclosure like storm relief goods off of a hovering chopper lest you want to start a world war" of snakes. Your pet snakes getting hurt by another pet snake will not be a pretty picture.

Feeding will mean them in the same enclosure could spell mayhem and chaos which may even result in unintentional cannibalism. Here is where your keen observations, imagination and ingenuity come in. Some suggestions we have is placing the food of each of your garter snakes in a separate container and once all in, you can introduce each snake into each container. Remember each container need not be an expensive sort, but ones which are clean for each feeding.

Chapter Five: Nutrition and Feeding

If there are only a couple of snakes to feed in one enclosure then make sure that you have a place for each of them all. Position dishes on separate corners so they don't fight over once piece of meal when there is enough to go around. Do this by putting each container dish of their preferred food in a separate place in the enclosure.

You may opt to use tongs to introduce the food to your garter snakes instead of offering chow with your bare fingers. We give a couple of more suggestions of how to feed them throughout the book, so you can check out and try some of these methods of feeding we suggest and learn a bit more on your own through experience. As you see the mere method and routine of feeding your garter snakes will take up a lot of your time and effort. Hence, be ready and committed.

Feeding Amount and Frequency

How often you feed your garter snakes is something you will definitely need to pencil in into your schedule. Juveniles will need to be fed at least once a day but the feeding ratio and frequency will both increase as they grow.

Feed newborn juveniles immediately. After that, you can schedule feeding your garter snakes two times every week if you are feeding it meal worms, earthworms and

Chapter Five: Nutrition and Feeding

night crawlers then you will have to set aside 2 weekly feeding schedules for each of the snakes. If you are feeding the garter snake a more nutritious fare like pinkies or fish, you can stick to a once a week feeding schedule for them.

Chapter Six: Maintenance for Garter Snakes

Keeping your garter snakes healthy is a very important part of what your everyday routine will look like. In order to raise healthy, well-tempered, awesome creatures, that they are, it is truly important for you to understand why keeping their habitat surroundings clean. Cleanliness is a big part of the reason for its complete wellness. And the opposite is the most common culprit for illness.

Reptiles have a defense mechanism of not showing illness or weakness, so be careful about keeping their habitat in pristine condition. To be called a responsible keeper of this striking creature it is vital that you are aware of what is needed of you in terms of time spent on maintaining the overall health care and wellness of your garter snakes. Your efforts and patience will play a big role in your garter snakes wellness. Read on and find out more.

Spot Cleaning Your Snake's Enclosure

Keep a journal. On this journal have separate sections that document each of the snakes traits and behaviors, what you feed them, any incidents and all observations. You will soon discover the convenience of being able to have information ready about your garter snakes should anything untoward arise.

One section of this journal would have to be a checklist of things you want to start making a habit of doing on a daily basis to make things easier for you and better for your pet snake's sake. That is checking each of the fittings, furnishing, temperature ranges and gradient, humidity level, water provision, substrate conditions and replacing anything that need to be restocked or replaced.

You want to make sure that there are no leftover foods that may lay under the substrate or land on the base of the enclosure hidden under it. Rotting food is an invitation for bacteria and fungi to fester and propagate. This will spell certain disaster for your pets which could make them sick. When a reptile is sick its immune system is weakend and it

Chapter Six: Maintenance for Garter Snakes

has a harder time fighting off malaise. So, make it a habit to visit with your snakes at least twice a day and have another responsible keeper stand in for you should you not be able to keep with routine. Here are some more reminders when cleaning your pet's cage:

- Make sure that temperature levels are at its most optimum, especially if you intend to breed them, if you have gravid females, during cold months - and hot for that matter.

- Make sure that their basking light is working fine and not emitting too much or too little heat. Keep in mind that keeping a garter snakes body temperature at its finest helps them with digestion and keeps their scales healthy and allow them to be the baskers they are.

- Heating pads allow them a warm corner of their enclosure to hide off to when other parts of the enclosure gets too cold.

- Humidity levels will be another thing you will want to make sure is at proper levels. Too much moisture can bring about skin and scale conditions in your garter snakes that may later deteriorate to worse cases. Constant or unchecked low humidity levels will make them pretty much dry out. So, it is very important that you keep the optimum level of each of these habitat enclosures at the right humidity level range.

Husbandry Tips and Guidelines on How to Clean Your Snake's Enclosure

Keep the habitat you created for your garter snakes at the most optimum temperature ranges not only to have it thrive properly doing so also allows them to have a better digestive system. Their habitat enclosure temperature should ideally be kept at a heat gradient of about 72 Fahrenheit on the cooler side. The warmer side of its habitat has to have a gradient temperature that ranges up to about 82 Fahrenheit.

Providing these thermal gradient areas allows them to regulate their body temperatures by moving from one side to another depending on what they would need at that particular time. You can use UV lights, firmly and sturdily affixed to one side of the habitat enclosure. Heating pads would also be another option that you can experiment on and check out because it should ideally work the same way.

Water is life! How many times have we heard this? Too many times and why that is because of the world of

Chapter Six: Maintenance for Garter Snakes

truth it holds. SO it is for your garter snake. You need to be able to provide a good shallow dish or bowl, with the proper amount of water for your garter snake to swim and bath in, and where it can drink from as well.

Desiccation can be a gradual condition the garter snake can experience if not given the correct amount of water it needs to hydrate itself and its skin. Essentially what this means is that the temperature the snake is exposed to, whether that is too cold or too hot, gives way for it to dry up. Make sure that the substrate you use is optimal for your garter snakes. Some very effective substrate suggestions of seasoned garter snake keepers are peanut shells and dry leaves during brumation period. Other substrates that work are newspaper pellets, shavings of aspen, paper pulp and wood pellets.

Apart from the daily checkup of the machinery hooked up to the enclosure, you will also want to make a weekly habit of checking out substrate conditions. The most optimum and also most expensive substrate is cypress shavings. Cypress shavings needn't be assisted with sprinkled or sprayed on water to keep it moisturized as cypress has enough moisture.

Use substrates like newspaper, not only are they easily available, but cheap and sometimes if you are resourceful enough - free! Other sorts of affordable and readily available acceptable substrates would be cage carpet which can be bought in most pet stores or online reptile habitat furnishing sellers. Not only does it make your colorful garter snakes color pop out vividly, cage carpet also allows you to instantly see snake droppings unlike substrate where feces can fall through.

Illnesses caused by Unsanitary and Unhealthy Living Conditions

Most illnesses in all living beings can stem and does begin from unkempt living conditions. It is so important that your snakes be in areas that will make them thrive instead of sick. A snake that has difficulty shedding could be in dehydrated. Dehydration is an avoidable situation which you will need to mind. Dysecdysis is a condition where a snake has a rough time shedding off skin.

Mites and ticks are usually carried by wild caught garter snakes and if these snakes get into contact with your captive bred snakes it could eat up a good portion of your time because you will have to manually pull them out with tweezers. Not only that you would have exposed the clean "ones" with the snake infested with pests.

Chapter Six: Maintenance for Garter Snakes

Moisture from substrate not changed often is considered to be poor conditions for garter snakes as these lead to skin blisters and skin infections. Keeping the surrounding habitat of your garter snakes gives them not only a great chance for a good life of health, it also allows you a measure of quiet success knowing that you do what you should be doing, as expected from any responsible herp aficionado. Snakes can also get a cold. If the habitat is too cold or wet, these conditions could make for a sick garter snake. You may hear the usual signs like wheezing, sneezing.

Chapter Six: Maintenance for Garter Snakes

Chapter Seven: Dealing and Handling Your Garter Snakes

You will find that dealing with garter snakes is actually very easy because their docile demeanor do half the job is not most of it for you. Remember that these little guys are big squirmier, so you will have to be ready to catch up with them. Show them off, go ahead. But do avoid handing them over to someone squeamish lest they be dropped or get into an accident.

They are not coilers, like other snakes are instead they slide and slither so easily from place to place which means they are very quick movers - real thrashers, if you may. So

Chapter Seven: Dealing & Handling Your Garter Snakes

when handling your snake, handle them on a table where, should it get away from you, you can reach out for it before it disappears. You want to be able to be fast enough for them because you wouldn't want to accidentally drop them and have them escape from you, unless you have time to kill and look for the little guy. In general garter snakes are pretty docile and agreeable when being handled - even those in the wild! But there are always going to be exceptions.

The columbrids are wired to emit a musky scent when spooked or agitated. They are gifted with this defense mechanism to ward of possible predators and to protect themselves when they feel threatened. This offending, smelly scent is given off from its vent (much like a fart). Once the garter snake gets used to you this will become less and less of a problem. It does happen, just pop into the bathroom and wash it off.

Yes, even these little guys can bite, and yes, the garter snake's saliva does contain minimal toxin that may cause certain people who are bit to have an allergic reaction. This is not a cause for too much concern (however a bite is a bite and can sting for a bit). Let's move on to discuss how to avoid these natural defensive reactions of the garter snake and find out how to properly deal with them.

Chapter Seven: Dealing & Handling Your Garter Snakes

Dealing With and Taming Your Garter Snake

You've read us say it and if you have been knee deep in your research about garter snakes then you would know how uncomplicated it is to tame one. There are tons of videos online which would attest to the fact that garter snakes are indeed some of the easiest going, actively curious, and friendliest of colmbrids.

Frequent socialization is really the only way to tame your garter snake. As you get to know each individual, each of your garter snake will get to know you too. You will find that with the many generalizations we make about any specie, each individual of any particular specie does have a personality of its own. When a skittish garter snake, a great escape artist too, becomes too fast for you and gives you a scare it may run off, you want to be a little more patient with this one. Allow them to come to you for a change.

Be consistent about letting them know of your presence from behind their habitat enclosure and see if they respond any differently - being more at ease - in time. You can also be a little more prepared for its movements and employ safety measures to avoid it from escaping from your grip.

Chapter Seven: Dealing & Handling Your Garter Snakes

Food seems to be a great way to make friends with a jumpy garter snake. Placing food in a container and then introducing the snake into the container during feeding time will allow you to be associated with food. And you know how food brings relationships together.

Taming Your Garter Snake

You want to establish your person and allow them to soften up to you on their own terms especially if they are the type who spooks easily. Keep in mind that garter snakes can just be as curious as you are of them, so allow them some space and be cautious.

Wash your hands before and after handling a snake. You don't want to transfer or exchange germs or bacteria with your garter snake. Do not move in and try to grab your snake, instead be deliberate, gentle and slow when picking up your snake. Avoid this altogether if the snake seems agitated and hisses at you. You can try again the next day. Let them know you are in the room by gently talking to them. Your voice and tone allows your presence to get established in the daily life of the garter snake.

As your snake gets to know you better and allows your hand to get closer you may try to pick it up. Do not

Chapter Seven: Dealing & Handling Your Garter Snakes

make the mistake of having to reset trust by picking the snake from its tail or its head. Snakes are sensitive about being head handled, especially when there is a certain amount of pressure involved. It is very vital to support your snake's body when you are picking or handling it up so that it is comfortable with you and there is no strain put on its body. This is true whether you are picking your snake up with your hands or with a hook. Keep the first third of your snake's body supported with either the hook or one of your hands, while supporting the back two thirds of your snake body with your other arm.

Keep in mind your hook training before putting your hands in your terrarium. Lightly pressing down on your snake's head with a hook will give the snake an idea that it is not feeding time so there is no need to strike. If your snake appears to be scared whenever you open its terrarium, spend a little more time rubbing its body with the hook until it calms down. If your snake coils into a ball, flatten out its body or pose a striking position, spend some time rubbing its body until it comes to a point that it will relax a bit.

You can start by rubbing your snake's body down from its tail end and up to its head. It could seem threatening if you start it with its head especially if your snake is already scared. Until you know within yourself that you can properly handle your snake, it is a good idea to hold

Chapter Seven: Dealing & Handling Your Garter Snakes

it with its head facing away from you. This will give your snake a chance to become familiar with the motion of your hands or body without risking to get bitten. Restraining your snake's head can make it believe that you are a predator that's trying to hurt the snake. Whenever you handle your snake, stick to holding it by its body, and avoid holding or restraining its head.

When it comes to dealing with aggression, the first thing to do is to know what type of aggression your snake is showing. There are two types of aggressive responses you can de-program your snake. It can either be territorial or defensive responses and feeding responses, these are instinctive and not an expression of aggressions. Snakes live most of their lives in fear, since they are always being preyed at by some bigger creatures, including humans, so this kind of response is more of a defense mechanism which can be tamed with gentle and consistent care.

Some species of garter snake could be more aggressive than others and might be requiring more training. If you're dealing with a particularly aggressive type of, you might consider training it by using a hook. You can do this by gently rubbing its body or pushing down on its head with a hook or a similar inanimate object, every time you go to get it out of its cage. By doing this, your snake will be able to know it is not yet feeding time so there is no need

Chapter Seven: Dealing & Handling Your Garter Snakes

to bite whatever enters its terrarium. Feeding responses are also a natural and instinctive response. Snakes in general are biologically programed to bite whatever comes into their terrarium. Since they assume that anything that comes to their cage is food, you might get bitten if you put your hand inside without first deprogramming this aggressive response.

People get bitten by their pet snake mostly because their snake is reacting to its feeding response every time something enters its terrarium. To handle this kind of response, stop feeding your snake every week. Instead, feed it only once every three weeks, but be sure to handle your snake every day. This will deprogram your pet from thinking that everything that enters its terrarium is food. It can also be useful to feed your snake in a separate tub. This will also help it from thinking that everything that comes to its terrarium is food.

Chapter Seven: Dealing & Handling Your Garter Snakes

Chapter Eight: Breeding Your Garter Snakes

Preparing to breed garter snakes? If you are then be ready. Garter snakes when birthed come aplenty. A little could be as small as 5 to more over 25. This number really depends on the size of the female garter snake. Remember to be ready because garter snakes multiply fast and many. You never know how many snakes a gravid female will yield, so always have a backup plan - such as breeding for an interested, experienced or potential herp looking for your sort of garter snake. Or perhaps you just want to multiply your own collection therefore be ready with extra enclosures. At any rate be ready for the results.

Chapter Eight: Breeding Your Garter Snakes

In the wild males come out from brumation and prepare themselves a little earlier than the females. Once the females are ready to mate and come out of months of inactivity, things start to happen. You will see a lot of activity and movement especially from the males. Male garter snakes can mate with two or more females. Hence, under captivity and your care the possibilities of having more than one gravid female are very probable. Ask yourself if this is what you want early on. Not only having more snakes than you can handle on your own be irresponsible it could also overwhelm you and put a real dent in your monthly and annual finances. On the other hand if this is indeed your purpose, then you should be able to prepare for all the things you would need for them. You will certainly need more terrariums than you originally had. You would need to prepare feeding containers where you can individually feed the juvenile garter snakes.

Sexual Dimorphism and Behavior

Unlike other snake species that a have very little, in fact almost no difference in terms of identification, visible physical differences of a male from a female one, garter snakes are quite the opposite. Most snakes' species is hard to sex just by looking at them. They would usually be sexed under the hand of an experienced reptile or snake vet and

Chapter Eight: Breeding Your Garter Snakes

undergo a pretty uncomfortable procedure of inspecting inside their cloaca. Evolution has it so that females are physically bigger than the more active, more slender bodied garter snake because female garters birth babies live. Yes, they come out a-squirming. While the lithe, more slender males are the way they are because they literally spend most of their time chasing after females.

How to Set Up the Right Breeding Conditions

Garter snakes begin brumation late in the year, early November. During this time garter snakes would typically be enclosed together in a brumation box with temperatures regulated to a very low degree. Try to mimic the temperature ranges that would occur naturally in nature would be one sure fire way of helping out captive breeding to happen.

You want to start off by giving the snakes their last food before brumation. Keep in mind that you want the food they ingest for the last time this season be digested well and should not stay in the intestinal tracts of the snakes. Food rot is a reality of undigested food. So help your snake's digestion along with the temperature control.

Chapter Eight: Breeding Your Garter Snakes

As winter enters the picture, your garter snakes would have ideally defecated the last food it has ingested and would naturally start the brumation process. Although they do not eat as much (or at all) during this time, hydrating them is still very important.

You want to put them in enclosure together and lay it with substrate like peanut shells, damp leaves or sawdust which you would slightly moisten with spritzes of water to keep the substrate in the enclosure humid. Make sure that you do not over moisturize the brumation enclosure as this could cause skin problems to the snakes.

Brumation could last from 3 - 4 months and although most reptiles would get cues from nature to start brumation, if you live in areas of regions where it may be too cold or too hot, you will need the aid of thermal regulation in order to help lower the body temperature of the garter snakes gradually. During this time you will notice very little movement or activity from your garter snakes.

Brumation ends sometime March. Your snakes will get their cue from nature almost instinctively and you shall start seeing more and more activity from your snakes. You may now help raise the temperature levels of your snakes and you would notice male's chase after females with gusto and enthusiasm.

Chapter Eight: Breeding Your Garter Snakes

Successful Garter Snake Breeding

Soon after coming out of brumation you will notice that males begin to feed almost immediately as long as the temperature in the enclosure is conducive. Generally, though you will notice that they would almost go at their food with gradual enthusiasm. This is especially true for pregnant females. It would usually be toward the first quarter of the year when you would notice the pregnant female become a little bigger around the belly area than it was. This signals a good breeding season.

You would normally see what would seem like a frenzied activity from about 25 - 30 male garter snakes copulate with a single female. Females produce a pheromone which attracts the males, and this would oftentimes intermingle with other snakes so it would not be surprising to see males on top of each other. This release of female pheromone instigates what looks like a fight over the ovulating female.

It is not unusual to see males coil and balled up together, engulfing each other in what would seem like a wrestling match of sorts. If you are lucky enough to chance upon mating garter snakes you would notice that males

Chapter Eight: Breeding Your Garter Snakes

would mount the females and coil their tails around the females not letting go until done with the deed.

Incubation of snakes is located in the lower abdomen of the gravid garter snake. They gestate in the entire length of the female's located abdomen until they are ready to be birthed around 2 to 3 months after the breeding season. Once a successful breeding has been compelled the females will go to find a quiet place where they can begin to care for themselves and the growing juveniles in their bellies.

The Birthing of Garters

We've mentioned that garter snakes are born live a few times earlier in this book which makes them ovoviviparous beings. Once the males and females come out of brumation they almost immediately copulate with males breeding with more than one female.

A couple or so months later the gravid female gives birth to live garter snakes that almost immediately shed. When it does the shed skin would seem to disappear almost immediately in minutes. As with most other animals who give birth to multiple offspring so it is the same for garter

Chapter Eight: Breeding Your Garter Snakes

snakes who may give birth to a litter of live squirming snakes numbering anywhere from 5 to 80!

These juveniles, come out like a small squirmy, shiny worm and almost immediately would hunt and feed on solid foods so this will be a very busy time for any garter snake breeder or keeper who has just had a gravid female give birth. The keeper would then have to step up to the plate introduce and provide the juveniles with the proper nutrition they would need.

It may be quite challenging and overwhelming to feed them all at this time, so be sure to have someone to help you out. Should you not be successful right away, don't give up and continue to keep attempting to feed the juvenile garter snakes as this is what your new born litter would need. Try to keep what they would do in captivity as close to their natural actions if they were in the wild.

It may take a while, even up to ten days before the juveniles take in what is offered to them. You want to start them off right away with the proper food they need. Offer them earthworm, meal or dew worms, pieces of cut up pinky mice. You may also lace pieces of the pinky mice with fish like silversides to entice them to feed if they are stubborn eaters.

Chapter Eight: Breeding Your Garter Snakes

Caring for Newborn and Juvenile Garter Snakes

Caring for garter snake babies is quite different from taking care of adult ones you have. Baby garter snakes, first of all need to be fed almost immediately after being birthed. This sounds easy enough but when you are inundated with an overwhelming number of tiny, little, quick and squirmy garter snakes all at the same time; it can be quite a daunting task to undertake on your own. You need to employ or ask for help at this time.

Baby garter snakes being much smaller should not have to be subjected to contend with food items bigger than them lest they choke and have to regurgitate the food. Not being able to eat because of the size of the "prey" of a baby garter snake could cause them to refuse to eat at all and lead to malnourishment.

Cut up pieces of thawed out acceptable food items like, earthworms, meal worms, pinkies and offer these to them. Make sure to separate each one during feeding and lay them back down in the habitat enclosure gently.

Baby garter snakes would also need a relatively higher moisture area for the first few weeks of its life. This next requirement calls for tedious and careful mindfulness

Chapter Eight: Breeding Your Garter Snakes

and may seem a bother, but it is vital if you want to have these babies survive and give them a fighting chance.

For the first few weeks of their lives you will have to separate them from the general population of the lot and make sure that their habitat enclosure is well moistened. Provide them with a substrate of damp shredded paper pellets or damp moss or mix them up. Baby garter snakes dehydrate quickly and equally overheat just as fast.

You want to first make sure that the habitat enclosure is well ventilated so that daily misting of the substrate can dry out a few hours later. It is ill advised to overly wet the substrate of the enclosure habitat as this could also lead to skin conditions like blisters. Overly dampened and ill ventilated habitats are great breeding grounds for bacteria and viruses that could make the snakes ill.

You can instead set out a shallow dish weighed down with pebbles and fill it to the middle and have this become a little pool where the snakes could take a quick dip or a fast sip of water. In addition to these keep the temperature range inside the separate habitat enclosure of the new baby garters at a temperature of 70 degrees Fahrenheit during night time. This temperature range allows the baby garter snakes to have better immunity development, better growth and it assists in their digestion of food. You can either place a

Chapter Eight: Breeding Your Garter Snakes

heating pad under another part of the habitat enclosure or use heated ceramic heating devices.

Life Cycle of a Garter Snake

Garter snakes from the get go the minute after being birthed alive and upon completion of the initial shed soon after emerging from the mother is immediately thrown into finding its own food. Since snakes do not have very good eyesight they are heavily reliant on their keen sense of smell. They pick on the scent an older garter snake may have taken on a previous hunt.

There is a divide on whether garter snakes are asocial or not. There are many captive garter snake owners who notice that garter snakes actually do enjoy being with their own sort most times of the year - these would be keepers who house their garter snakes in the same habitat/enclosure. And then there are those who choose to give their garter snakes separate habitat quarters and put them in the mix when it is mating season.

At any rate the initial stage of a garter snakes life cycle begins the moment it emerges from its mother a full blown juvenile snake. This is because this specie of snake is incubated inside the gravid female for a period of about 2 - 3

Chapter Eight: Breeding Your Garter Snakes

months. The eggs of the juveniles are hatched inside of the gravid female and so goes the process before live birth.

It becomes independent immediately after it is out in the world. In the wild a garter snake has a lot of outside and uncontrolled forces which dictate its longevity and survival in nature. One would be the presence of predators - an everyday reality these smaller columbrids face daily. Another factor would be the availability of food and the competition amongst other garter snakes and eaters of the same sort of food fare they prefer.

Illness and disease also is another factor that most wild animals have to endure in silence. All in all a wild garter snake has a good chance of living a span of about 4-5 years, with a marginal population existing a tad longer. When wild garter snakes are compared to captive garter snakes, the latter have a better advantage of living quite a longer existence of up to 10 or so years given the proper optimum care from its keeper.

Chapter Eight: Breeding Your Garter Snakes

Chapter Nine: Common Diseases and Treatments for Garter Snakes

As with other reptiles and amphibians, garter snakes have their own set of problems that could put them in undesirably bad health conditions. Knowledge is indeed power and learning has always been part of facts we know. We mentioned mites and ticks earlier as being one of the more tedious and possibly the peskiest of conditions garter snakes can get. Aside from this we have listed other garter snake issues which we hope you don't have to come across, but something you are prepared for. Be sure to ask your herp vet more questions because you will later on have some

Chapter Nine: Common Diseases and Treatments for Garter Snakes

quesries about your garter snakes that only seasoned experts can provide.

This chapter will talk about some of the health issues which could affect your garter snakes. We aim to enlighten you more a bit about the ailments which are commonly found in garter snakes. There are those which you can specifically avoid which you should be aware of giving you the upper hand of making sure that you are indeed givng your snake the best care. Some of them are avoidable and others treatable if detected early enough, so there is a ray of hope in some cases. Let's get on and find out what these are and what owner/keepers can do to avert these common diseases and ailments from plaguing your garter snakes.

Common Minor Problems

Healthy snakes will be able to shed their skin easily. Some simply slide out of their old skin revealing a new shiny suit. But those in poor habitat conditions may in fact experience this. Some garter snakes will show display some difficulty shedding their skins and may simply need a hand from you by pinning down part of the already shed skin so that the snake can slip out of it. However if you notice this in your garter snake then you will have to check on the humidity levels of your snakes enclosure.

Chapter Nine: Common Diseases and Treatments for Garter Snakes

You can help out by setting out bowl of water wherein the snake can pop in for a soak. You see most reptiles evolved with innate knowledge of what to do in some situations but have not control of healing themselves because of captivity ill provisions in human controlled habitats. Make sure that you set out a bowl halfway filled with water and allow it to soak in the water to soften its skin.

Garter snakes rely on their keen sense of smell and instinct by use of their two-toned tongues because they don't have pretty lousy eyesight. One reason for this is because snakes have scales which cover and protect their eyes since they do not blink. These look very similar to contact lenses when they are shed. When snakes get rid of their skin, the contact-lens like scales which protect their eyes is shed as well. However if your garter snake is facing the challenge of not getting enough moisture it would not only affect how it sheds it's skin, this would also hamper with the rejuvenation of the scales protecting the garter snake's eyes.

This can be very difficult for the garter snake and would need some help in getting them off. A seasoned herp vet would be needed in this case to manually remove the scales. Never employ tweezers as you may just accidentally poke out your very squirmy buddies eyes. You want to take it to someone experienced who can help with the removal. It

Chapter Nine: Common Diseases and Treatments for Garter Snakes

is also advisable that if possible, you watch what is done to your snake and learn the procedure as a precaution for later. Ideally what you want to do it to check on the humidity levels of the habitat enclosure of your garter snakes because you will usually find the reason and solution in there. So always remember to keep a shallow water bowl dish, half-filled with water in the habitat of the snakes because this allows their skin (over time) to loosen up and shed easier.

Lack of Appetite

We had been giving bit and pieces of vital information on how to feed your garter snake without injury to self, your pet or the other garter snake occupants of a habitat. With that in mind garter snakes are eager eaters and would almost launch themselves when feeding time comes around. When you notice the absence of eagerness to feed and loss of appetite, it could merely sometimes be as simple as their body clocks telling them that it is time to brumate. Once out of brumation you can start introducing food like pinkies for reasons you will read later in the next sections.

Some juveniles especially those who had just been born will not eat immediately so remember to refer back to our previous discussion on this matter.

Chapter Nine: Common Diseases and Treatments for Garter Snakes

Bister Disease

Again, in any circumstance which seems strange from the usual, the journal you keep on each of your pets will help you investigate back on the possible culprit. If you notice puffy sores on your snake's body the culprit for this condition could be high moisture levels in the habitat of the snake. Address this issue by keeping the habitat conditions of your snake in a drier state. Take the blister skinned snake to the herp vet to confirm the condition, diagnose and seek treatment and medication as soon as you can.

Vomiting and Regurgitation

Being the voracious eaters they are, sometimes garter snakes would take in and try to ingest more than they can handle, gobbling down big chunks of food items that later give them a hard time digesting. One possible solution is to cut up the food you offer them. Other causes of regurgitation could be infections of various sorts, drinking large amounts of water right after a meal, food items that are too big for a small snake, dehydration, immediate handling after a meal, or eating a meal with feet, backward. Food that are toxic and are given on a frequent basis could also be the reason for this event of upchucking food. But you also want to look into the temperature of the habitat. Remember that when the

Chapter Nine: Common Diseases and Treatments for Garter Snakes

temperature of a reptile, especially snake's, habitat is too low; it gives the snake a harder time to digest its food. When not able to digest properly, food rot incidences in garter snakes increases incrementally.

Other times regurgitation happens because of too much stress and movement in its habitat enclosure and could be as simple as introducing a new snake into the habitat. So make sure that patience is observed when socializing your snakes. You need to recognize if a recent feeding would have been the cause for the snake to regurgitate its food. Being the little guys that they are with big appetites they could voraciously attack a larger piece of food and not be able to digest all of it properly. Over-feeding them is another issue that you want to look out.

Vomiting on the other hand could be a greater cause of concern as this can signal internal problems. The presence of bacteria in its habitat could be the reason for this medical concern. Check that you are religiously and routinely cleaning out its habitat enclosure to avoid bacteria from nesting and flourishing in its ecosystem

Common Major Problems

Chapter Nine: Common Diseases and Treatments for Garter Snakes

Garter snakes can come across some pretty dire health problems if not given the optimal diet it needs. It cannot get too much or too little of one food fare or another - whether they are the acceptable ones (more so, if not). But there are ways to make sure that the garter snake won't be as exposed or too prone to these diseases given a few rules to follow with its husbandry and maintenance.

Food and habitat need to be checked first off. You want to make sure that you either get food from reputable bait and reptile feed sellers whose business is to not only sell these products but that their food catches are of sound harvesting and safe for your garter snake.

Lack of Vitamin B1

Another culprit for health problems does also stem from lack of dietary balance. One fatal condition, if not known early and corrected as soon as possible, is thiamin deficiency. Simply put thiamine deficiency is the lack of Vitamin B1 in your garter snake. A garter fish on a sole fish diet can develop Vitamin B1 deficiency because many of the fish fed to garter snakes contain thiamine. This enzyme present in most fish is the leading cause of the absence of vitamin B1. You need not rid your pet snake completely of the fish in its diet but you do want to limit it or completely

Chapter Nine: Common Diseases and Treatments for Garter Snakes

eliminate it from its food fare choices. You may reset you garter snake's diet after brumation and start introducing pinkies.

Supplementing the fish food with powdered vitamin B1 would be an exercise in futility even if you do since thiamine is present in most of them and freezing does not rid the fish of the enzyme and it would still breakdown any properties of vitamin B1 supplement you add.

Other Health Issues

Some major problems in garter snakes mostly stem from improper temperature settings, unsuitable food and unkempt habitats. When these are ignored and left to chance, conditions of the garter snake could silently fester with no manifestation until it is a serious condition. This is an opportune time to remind you of the importance of providing your garter snakes an optimally balanced meal. Avoid foods that would pave the way for any vitamin deficiencies and internal parasites.

Garter snakes which die in captivity for no apparent reason is not only heartbreaking but also alarming, this is why many experienced herps who have lost pet garters have learnt that dietary choices they give their garter snakes - no matter how well meaning - could sometimes be the cause of

Chapter Nine: Common Diseases and Treatments for Garter Snakes

illness in the snake. Garter snakes have a tendency to be quite susceptible to internal parasite infestation because of the diet they have. Live fish, amphibians caught in the wild, and earthworms are carriers of parasites and all of them are probable carriers.

Internal parasites could be living organisms like viruses, and bacteria. The carriers like pin worms, tapeworms could dig their way under the skin of your garter snake and live there! These parasites are not easy to detect until they are obvious on the skin of the garter snake. They would usually manifest themselves to be lumps under the skin. If you notice this in your snake, you need to immediately take your garter snake to the herp vet.

The herp vet would then attempt to surgically remove the parasite burrowed under its skin, and if caught early would be a simple procedure of removal. Serious cases have been documented of internal parasites not detected in snakes hence more fatal results have become the outcome of these situations. Roundworms, tin worms and tapeworms have actually been surgically harvested and removed from infected snake's bodies without incident. Other times, these worms can work their way into the vital organs of a garter snake and cause greater havoc on its health.

Chapter Nine: Common Diseases and Treatments for Garter Snakes

Solutions we collated from experienced vets and seasoned herp vets would suggest routine and frequent deworming of your garter snake. Notice how we say routine and frequent deworming, because these parasites do reoccur at any given time. Others would say that feeding your garter snakes thawed out mice which had been in frozen storage for 30 days could minimize the problem.

If you can and are successful in training your garter snake to eat frozen food like fish, pinkies, mice and the worms (mealworms, earthworms, slugs) the chances of them getting internal parasites could considerably lessen. Remember that your diligence and patience will only help increase the chances of your garter snakes surviving these early stages of their lives. Do not be disheartened if you lose a few of them as this is just the way things normally work for any specie born together in larger than usual numbers.

Chapter Ten: Garter Snake Summary

As we close this book we hope that you have gathered more than enough information to be able to come to ask yourself the tougher question of "am I ready to handle the financial and daily maintenance responsibilities which entail owning garter snakes?"

Your time will certainly have to be divided from what you regularly do so be aware of this and factor in your lifestyle and assess whether you are ready to head down the road of being responsible for a group of colourfully active, daytime, players who if taken care of correctly can be a joy to behold.

Chapter Ten: Garter Snake Summary

Well, you have come to the end of our little book on the compilation of details and requirements needed by garter snakes. We hope that your learning is extended beyond this period and you enjoy the company of your tiny slithers for a long time.

Points to Remember

- They're found in New Mexico, Oregon, and Mississippi. There are others that call Chicago their home. You will also find many garter snakes in Texas. A number of them are indigenous to areas like the Hernando County in Florida. There are also those found in the eastern part of the Florida Gulf coast. Others call the coastal area of the Pacific Northwest, namely Washington, their home. Garter snakes have also been imported overseas, like Sweden and Canada.

- They range in length depending on their specie but the most common ones are about 22 to 54 inches and weigh an average of about 5.5 ounces.

Chapter Ten: Garter Snake Summary

Kinds of Garter Snake

- **Eastern Garter Snake**

  It is named such because of its strap - like appearance; the Eastern Garter Snake is a New Latin term because of its striped pattern look. It averages a length of about 18-24 inches with females out-lengthening males.

- **Red-Spotted Garter Snakes**

  This subspecies of the garter snake is a compelling vision with its deep ebony base scales, and a red spotted cranium. These garter snakes call the marshes and damp lands of Western Oregon.

- **San Fransisco Garter Snake**

  They are a native of central western part of California, particularly in the San Mateo County in the brackish estuaries of San Francisco. It is protected and has sadly been listed as endangered by the law since 1969 which means that it is illegal to keep or purvey them.

- **Santa Cruz Garter Snake**

  These snakes found in the ranges of California and Oregon. They are a subspecies that amazingly color morphs from a sole line of strip to 3 strips which run down its back.

- **Bluestripe Garter Snakes**
Bluestripe garter snakes get their moniker from the blue stripes which are found on their spine as well as dorsal scales just above the stomach of their graceful bodies. This garter snake matures to an average length of about 26 inches and the maximum length of a bluestripe garter snake was recorded to be close to 40 inches!

- **The Mexican Garter Snake**
The Mexican Garter Snake used to slither aplenty in numbers in the Arizona. Measuring in at 44 inches, they come in olive-brown color, while others sport a reddish-brown color with a creamy stripe trailing its back

- **Valley Garter Snake**
They are usually found in the many basins of California and their range is wide from Siskiyou County, Sacramento County, the foothills of Sierra Nevada, and North Humboldt County.

Chapter Ten: Garter Snake Summary

- **California Red – sided Garter Snake**

    It occurs in a wide range of the basins and valleys as well as the marsh and wet lands of California. The red-sided garter snakes have relatively bigger eyes than other garter snakes and averages 38 inches.

- **Puget Sound Garter Snake**

    This red flecked sided snake native of the regions of Washington and it grows up to about a meter long.

What Makes It a Great Pet

- They are not aggressive and are usually accepting of frequent handling by their owners. Garter snakes get along relatively well with other snakes when housed together with those who are not snake-eaters

- When housed together with their sort and kind you will find them actively social with each other.

- They like to huddle together during cold winter months and "steal" warmth from each other and keep each other company.

Chapter Ten: Garter Snake Summary

- Given that the traits of the other snake specie are peaceful and agreeable to having other snake specie for company

Pros and Cons of Garter Snakes

- They are pretty mild mannered and would just be happy to be in a terrarium or vivarium that would mimic their natural habitat.

- Their saliva does have properties toxic to their prey but are harmless to humans.

- A downside we can think of is being surprised by the number of live snakes a gravid female can give birth to if an owner is not knowledgeable of the gravid and birthing process of garter snakes.

Habitat Requirements for Garter Snakes

- Remember that there is a difference between an enclosure and a habitat. A habitat is what you will have to research, design and imagine as you carry out the task of fashioning a living space that would closely mimic the garter snakes natural environment. We are sure that because of your excitement to see

Chapter Ten: Garter Snake Summary

these beauties in their full glory, the habitat you will make for them will be even better than what conditions they have out in the wild. An enclosure is simply what it is - a plain old cage.

- Be sure that you sanitize not only the enclosure of the snakes but that you put in sanitized and fresh furnishings of climbing branches, logs to crawl up or through which can also double as hides. Remember to always make enough hides for the occupants of the tank to be able to rest whenever they feel like it.

Nutritional Requirements

- You now know that there are a number of acceptable food and others that aren't by a garter snake. Make sure to never overfeed or underfeed them and to have them each get the proper amount of nutrients without skimping on balance.

- Be reminded that you will need to feed any juveniles birthed under your care whether these juveniles were intended to be bred or not. Make sure that you are in touch with your herp expert vet to understand other details about your garter snakes which you may have.

Chapter Ten: Garter Snake Summary

Maintenance for Garter Snakes

- A clean habitat is essential in relation to a healthy and balanced wellness of a garter snake. Most illnesses come from shoddily kept habitat enclosures that are neglected or left to be dirty.

- Keep in mind the food quality you will be feeding your new garter snakes and make sure to network with recently successful garter snake breeders to get the low down on where to get proper feeding items which are free of pesticides and is not laden with any form of toxicity that could pose certain danger for your garter snakes.

Guidelines on How to Clean Your Garter Snake's Enclosure

- Consider that journal of events on your garter snake seriously. And make checklists for items, devices, machinery that you would need to check for consistently that these are in proper operational use and fit for the habitat of the feisty little columbrids.

- Having a visible and posted checklist and running down through the list one by one as you walk

Chapter Ten: Garter Snake Summary

through your reptile den allows you to confidently form the habit of making sure that all equipment especially those that provide gradient heating temperature, humidity level reader, UV lamps and heating or ceramic pads are properly in working order.

- You want to check the condition of the substrate and make sure that there are no food remnants that can rot away and cause illness to spread amongst the population in that habitat enclosure.

Dealing and Handling Your Garter Snakes

- Be sure that you are patient and gentle with your snakes. Be consistent about getting to know them.

- Talk to them softly and establish yourself as a friend and not a foe.

- Make sure that you are well aware of each of them and that you get to know each of your garter snakes on an individual level.

Chapter Ten: Garter Snake Summary

Breeding Process of Garter Snakes

- Try to mimic the temperature ranges that would occur naturally in nature would be one sure fire way of helping out captive breeding to happen.

- You want to start off by giving the snakes their last food before brumation.

- You want to put them in enclosure together and lay it with substrate like peanut shells, damp leaves or sawdust which you would slightly moisten with spritzes of water to keep the substrate in the enclosure humid.

- Brumation could last from 3 - 4 months, during this time you will notice very little movement or activity from your garter snakes.

- Once the males and females come out of brumation they almost immediately copulate with males breeding with more than one female.

- These juveniles, come out like a small squirmy, shiny worm and almost immediately would hunt and feed on solid foods; Offer them earthworm, meal or dew worms, pieces of cut up pinky mice.

Chapter Ten: Garter Snake Summary

- For the first few weeks of their lives you will have to separate them from the general population of the lot and make sure that their habitat enclosure is well moistened.

- Provide them with a substrate of damp shredded paper pellets or damp moss or mix them up.

- Keep the temperature range inside the separate habitat enclosure of the new baby garters at a temperature of 70 degrees Fahrenheit during night time.

Common Diseases and Solutions

- **Lack of Appetite:** When you notice the absence of eagerness to feed and loss of appetite, it could merely sometimes be as simple as their body clocks telling them that it is time to brumate. Some juveniles especially those who had just been born will not eat immediately.

- **Bister Disease:** If you notice puffy sores on your snake's body the culprit for this condition could be high moisture levels in the habitat of the snake. Address this issue by keeping the habitat conditions of your snake in a drier state.

Chapter Ten: Garter Snake Summary

- **Vomiting and Regurgitation: If your** garter snakes try to ingest more than they can handle, gobbling down big chunks of food items that later give them a hard time digesting, it can result to regurgitation. One possible solution is to cut up the food you offer them. Vomiting on the other hand could be a greater cause of concern as this can signal internal problems.

- **Lack of Vitamin B1:** thiamine deficiency is the lack of Vitamin B1 in your garter snake. It's usually caused by fish that contains thiamine; You need not rid your pet snake completely of the fish in its diet but you do want to limit it or completely eliminate it from its food fare choices.

- **Internal Parasites**: Internal parasites could be living organisms like viruses, and bacteria. If you notice this in your snake, you need to immediately take your garter snake to the herp vet.

Glossary of Snake Terms

1.2.3. (Numbers with full stops) – The numbers are used to denote the number of a species, arranged according to sex, thus: male.female.unknown sex. In this case, one male, two females, and three of unknown sex.

Acclimation – Adjusting to a new environment or new conditions over a period of time.

Active range – The area of activity which can include hunting, seeking refuge, and finding a mate.

Ambient temperature – The overall temperature of the environment.

Amelanistic – Amel for short; without melanin, or without any black or brown coloration.

Anal Plate – A modified ventral scale that covers and protects the vent; sometimes a single plate, sometimes a divided plate.

Anerythristic – Anery for short; without any red coloration.

Aquatic – Lives in water.

Arboreal – Lives in trees.

Betadine – An antiseptic that can be used to clean wounds in reptiles.

Bilateral – Where stripes, spots or markings are present on both sides of an animal.

Biotic – The living components of an environment.

Brille – A transparent scale above the eyes of snakes that allows them to see but also serves to protect the eyes at the same time. Also called Spectacle, and Ocular Scale.

Brumation – The equivalent of mammalian hibernation among reptiles.

Cannibalistic – Where an animal feeds on others of its own kind.

Caudocephalic Waves – The ripple-like contractions that move from the rear to the front of a snake's body.

CB – Captive Bred, or bred in captivity.

CH – Captive Hatched.

Cloaca – also Vent; a half-moon shaped opening for digestive waste disposal and sexual organs.

Cloacal Gaping – Indication of sexual receptivity of the female.

Cloacal Gland – A gland at the base of the tail which emits foul smelling liquid as a defense mechanism; also called Anal Gland.

Clutch – A batch of eggs.

Constriction – The act of wrapping or coiling around a prey to subdue and kill it prior to eating.

Crepuscular – Active at twilight, usually from dusk to dawn.

Crypsis – Camouflage or concealing.

Diurnal – Active by day

Drop – To lay eggs or to bear live young.

Ectothermic – Cold-blooded. An animal that cannot regulate its own body temperature, but sources body heat from the surroundings.

Endemic – Indigenous to a specific region or area.

Estivation – Also Aestivation; a period of dormancy that usually occurs during the hot or dry seasons in order to escape the heat or to remain hydrated.

Faunarium (Faun) – A plastic enclosure with an air holed lid, usually used for small animals such as hatchling snakes, lizards, and insects.

FK – Fresh Killed; a term usually used when feeding a rodent that is recently killed, and therefore still warm, to a pet snake.

Flexarium – A reptile enclosure that is mostly made from mesh screening, for species that require plenty of ventilation.

Fossorial – A burrowing species.

Fuzzy – For rodent prey, one that has just reached the stage of development where fur is starting to grow.

F/T – Frozen/thawed; used to refer to food items that are frozen but thawed before feeding to your pet.

Gestation – The period of development of an embryo within a female.

Gravid – The equivalent of pregnant in reptiles.

Glottis – A tube-like structure that projects from the lower jaw of a snake to facilitate ingestion of large food items.

Gut-loading – Feeding insects within 24 hours to a prey before they are fed to your pet, so that they pass on the nutritional benefits.

Hatchling – A newly hatched, or baby, reptile.

Hemipenes – Dual sex organs; common among male snakes.

Hemipenis – A single protrusion of a paired sexual organ; one half is used during copulation.

Herps/Herpetiles – A collective name for reptile and amphibian species.

Herpetoculturist – A person who keeps and breeds reptiles in captivity.

Herpetologist – A person who studies ectothermic animals, sometimes also used for those who keeps reptiles.

Herpetology – The study of reptiles and amphibians.

Hide Box – A furnishing within a reptile cage that gives the animal a secure place to hide.

Hots – Venomous.

Husbandry – The daily care of a pet reptile.

Hygrometer – Used to measure humidity.

Impaction – A blockage in the digestive tract due to the swallowing of an object that cannot be digested or broken down.

Incubate – Maintaining eggs in conditions favorable for development and hatching.

Interstitial – The skin between scales.

Intromission – Also mating; when the male's hemipenis is inserted into the cloaca of the female.

Juvenile – Not yet adult; not of breedable age.

LTC – Long Term Captive; or one that has been in captivity for more than six months.

MBD – Metabolic Bone Disease; occurs when reptiles lack sufficient calcium in their diet.

Morph – Color pattern

Musking – Secretion of a foul smelling liquid from its vent as a defense mechanism.

Oviparous – Egg-bearing.

Ovoviviparous – Eggs are retained inside the female's body until they hatch.

Pinkie – Newborn rodent.

Pip – The act of a hatchling snake to cut its way out of the egg using a special egg tooth.

PK – Pre-killed; a term used when live rodents are not fed to a snake.

Popping – The process by which the sex is determined among hatchlings.

Probing – The process by which the sex is determined among adults.

Regurgitation – Also Regurge; occurs when a snake regurgitates or brings out a half-digested meal.

R.I. – Respiratory Infection; common condition among reptiles kept in poor conditions.

Serpentine Locomotion – The manner in which snakes move.

Sloughing – Shedding.

Sub-adult – Juvenile.

Substrate – The material lining the bottom of a reptile enclosure.

Stat – Short for Thermostat

Tag – Slang for a bite or being bitten

Terrarium – A reptile enclosure.

Thermo-regulation – The process by which cold-blooded animals regulate their body temperature by moving from hot to cold surroundings.

Vent – Cloaca

Vivarium – Glass-fronted enclosure

Viviparous – Gives birth to live young.

WC – Wild Caught.

Weaner – A sub-adult rodent.

WF – Wild Farmed; refers to the collection of a pregnant female whose eggs or young were hatched or born in captivity.

Yearling – A year old.

Zoonosis – A disease that can be passed from animal to man.

Index

$

$15-25 90

1

1.2.3. (Numbers with full stops) – The numbers are used to denote the number of a species, arranged according to sex, thus
male.female.unknown sex. In this case, one male, two females, and three of unknown sex. 85

A

Cloaca – also Vent 86
Estivation – Also Aestivation 87
PK – Pre-killed 90
FK – Fresh Killed 87
Acclimation – Adjusting to a new environment or new conditions over a period of time. 85
Active range – The area of activity which can include hunting, seeking refuge, and finding a mate. 85
Cloacal Gland – A gland at the base of the tail which emits foul smelling liquid as a defense mechanism 86
Ambient temperature – The overall temperature of the environment. 85
Aquatic – Lives in water. 85
Arboreal – Lives in trees. 85

B

Betadine – An antiseptic that can be used to clean wounds in reptiles. 85
Bilateral – Where stripes, spots or markings are present on both sides of an animal. ... 86
Biotic – The living components of an environment. 86

Brille – A transparent scale above the eyes of snakes that allows them to see but also serves to protect the eyes at the same time. Also called Spectacle, and Ocular Scale. 86

Brumation – The equivalent of mammalian hibernation among reptiles. 86

C

Cannibalistic – Where an animal feeds on others of its own kind. 86

Caudocephalic Waves – The ripple-like contractions that move from the rear to the front of a snake's body. 86

CB – Captive Bred, or bred in captivity. 86

CH – Captive Hatched. 86

Cloacal Gaping – Indication of sexual receptivity of the female. 86

Clutch – A batch of eggs. 86

Hemipenes – Dual sex organs 88

R.I. – Respiratory Infection 90

Constriction – The act of wrapping or coiling around a prey to subdue and kill it prior to eating. 87

Crepuscular – Active at twilight, usually from dusk to dawn. 87

Crypsis – Camouflage or concealing. 87

D

Diurnal – Active by day 87

Drop – To lay eggs or to bear live young. 87

E

Ectothermic – Cold-blooded. An animal that cannot regulate its own body temperature, but sources body heat from the surroundings. 87

Endemic – Indigenous to a specific region or area. 87

F

Faunarium (Faun) – A plastic enclosure with an air holed lid, usually used for small animals such as hatchling snakes, lizards, and insects. 87

Flexarium – A reptile enclosure that is mostly made from mesh screening, for species that require plenty of ventilation. 87
Fossorial – A burrowing species. 87
Fuzzy – For rodent prey, one that has just reached the stage of development where fur is starting to grow. 88

G

Gestation – The period of development of an embryo within a female. 88
Glottis – A tube-like structure that projects from the lower jaw of a snake to facilitate ingestion of large food items. 88
Gravid – The equivalent of pregnant in reptiles. 88
Gut-loading – Feeding insects within 24 hours to a prey before they are fed to your pet, so that they pass on the nutritional benefits. 88

H

Hatchling – A newly hatched, or baby, reptile. 88
Herpetoculturist – A person who keeps and breeds reptiles in captivity. 88
Herpetologist – A person who studies ectothermic animals, sometimes also used for those who keeps reptiles. 88
Herpetology – The study of reptiles and amphibians. 88
Herps/Herpetiles – A collective name for reptile and amphibian species. 88
Hide Box – A furnishing within a reptile cage that gives the animal a secure place to hide. 89
Hots – Venomous. 89
Husbandry – The daily care of a pet reptile. 89
Hygrometer – Used to measure humidity. 89

I

Impaction – A blockage in the digestive tract due to the swallowing of an object that cannot be digested or broken down. 89
Incubate – Maintaining eggs in conditions favorable for development and hatching. 89
Interstitial – The skin between scales. 89

M

Morph – Color pattern 89
Musking – Secretion of a foul smelling liquid from its vent as a defense mechanism 89

N

Juvenile – Not yet adult 89

O

Regurgitation – Also Regurge 90
MBD – Metabolic Bone Disease 89
Hemipenis – A single protrusion of a paired sexual organ 88
LTC – Long Term Captive 89
Oviparous – Egg-bearing. 89
Ovoviviparous – Eggs are retained inside the female's body until they hatch. 90

P

Pinkie – Newborn rodent. 90
Pip – The act of a hatchling snake to cut its way out of the egg using a special egg tooth. 90
Popping – The process by which the sex is determined among hatchlings. 90
Probing – The process by which the sex is determined among adults. 90

R

WF – Wild Farmed 91

S

Serpentine Locomotion – The manner in which snakes move. 90
Sloughing – Shedding. 90
Anal Plate – A modified ventral scale that covers and protects the vent 85
Stat – Short for Thermostat 90

Sub-adult – Juvenile. 90
Substrate – The material lining the bottom of a reptile enclosure. 90

T

Tag – Slang for a bite or being bitten..91
Terrarium – A reptile enclosure. 91
Thermo-regulation – The process by which cold-blooded animals regulate their body temperature by moving from hot to cold surroundings..91

U

F/T – Frozen/thawed 88

V

Vent – Cloaca 91
Vivarium – Glass-fronted enclosure 91
Viviparous – Gives birth to live young. 91

W

WC – Wild Caught. 91
Weaner – A sub-adult rodent. 91
Intromission – Also mating 89
Anerythristic – Anery for short 85
Amelanistic – Amel for short 85

Y

Yearling – A year old. 91

Photo Credits

Page 1 Photo by user brwnneyedgrl via Pixabay.com, https://pixabay.com/en/snake-blue-nature-animal-wild-2612906/

Page 3 Photo by user OlinEJ via Pixabay.com, https://pixabay.com/en/snake-tongue-garter-snake-reptile-2569669/

Page 15 Photo by user Kapa65 via Pixabay.com, https://pixabay.com/en/snake-young-animal-cute-slim-1556169/

Page 22 Photo by user tdfugere via Pixabay.com, https://pixabay.com/en/garter-snake-snake-reptile-garter-1264269/

Page 29 Photo by user WildOne via Pixabay.com, https://pixabay.com/en/snake-garter-reptile-wildlife-2401275/

Page 36 Photo by user skeeze via Pixabay.com, https://pixabay.com/en/garter-snakes-wildlife-nature-941321/

Page 42 Photo by user PublicDomainImages via Pixabay.com, https://pixabay.com/en/area-muddy-through-slithers-snake-387218/

Page 50 Photo by user svcostanzo via Pixabay.com, https://pixabay.com/en/snake-garter-snake-nature-serpent-296919/

Page 60 Photo by user paulket1968 via Pixabay.com, https://pixabay.com/en/snakes-reptiles-animal-wild-2790384/

Page 72 Photo by user PublicDomainImages via Pixabay.com, https://pixabay.com/en/snakes-reptiles-garter-family-18899/

Page 83 Photo by user jasonjdking via Pixabay.com, https://pixabay.com/en/common-garter-snake-snake-reptile-744785/

References

"Breeding and care in captivity of the Thamnophis atratus atratus" - Stevenbolgartersnakes.com

http://stevenbolgartersnakes.com/publications/breeding-and-care-in-captivity-of-the-santa-cruz-garter-snake-t-a-atratus-kennicott-1860/

"Common Garter Snake" - Wikipedia
https://en.wikipedia.org/wiki/Common_garter_snake

"Eastern Garter Snake" - Wikipedia
https://en.wikipedia.org/wiki/Eastern_garter_snake

"Garter Snake" - Wikipedia
https://en.wikipedia.org/wiki/Garter_snake#Species_and_subspecies

"Garter Snake Breeding" - ReptilesMagazine.com
http://www.reptilesmagazine.com/Reptile-Magazines/Reptiles-Magazine/May-2010/Breeding-Garter-Snakes/

"Garter Snake Care Sheet" - ReptilesMagazine.com
http://www.reptilesmagazine.com/Garter-Snake-Care-Sheet/

"Kleptothermy" - Wikipedia
https://en.wikipedia.org/wiki/Kleptothermy

"Mexican Gartersnake Thamnophis Eques" – Reptilesofaz.org
http://www.reptilesofaz.org/Snakes-Subpages/h-t-eques.html

"Living with Wildlife Snakes" – DFW State Organization
http://www.dfw.state.or.us/wildlife/living_with/docs/livingwsnakes.pdf

"San Francisco Garter Snake" - ReptilesMagazine.com
http://www.reptilesmagazine.com/Snake-Species/San-Francisco-Garter-Snake/

"Species" – Gartersnake Info
http://www.gartersnake.info/species/

"The Garter Snake" - ReptilesMagazine.com
http://www.reptilesmagazine.com/Garter-Snakes-For-Starters/

Feeding Baby
Cynthia Cherry
978-1941070000

Axolotl
Lolly Brown
978-0989658430

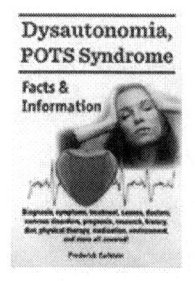

Dysautonomia, POTS Syndrome
Frederick Earlstein
978-0989658485

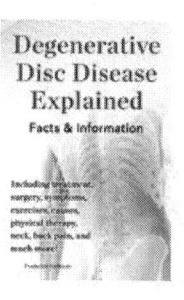

Degenerative Disc Disease Explained
Frederick Earlstein
978-0989658485

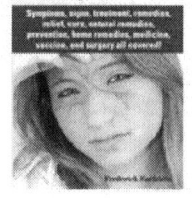

Sinusitis, Hay Fever,
Allergic Rhinitis Explained
Frederick Earlstein
978-1941070024

Wicca
Riley Star
978-1941070130

Zombie Apocalypse
Rex Cutty
978-1941070154

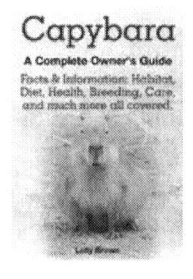

Capybara
Lolly Brown
978-1941070062

Eels As Pets
Lolly Brown
978-1941070167

Scabies and Lice Explained
Frederick Earlstein
978-1941070017

Saltwater Fish As Pets
Lolly Brown
978-0989658461

Torticollis Explained
Frederick Earlstein
978-1941070055

Kennel Cough
Lolly Brown
978-0989658409

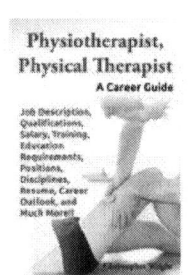

Physiotherapist, Physical Therapist
Christopher Wright
978-0989658492

Rats, Mice, and Dormice As Pets
Lolly Brown
978-1941070079

Wallaby and Wallaroo Care
Lolly Brown
978-1941070031

Bodybuilding Supplements
Explained
Jon Shelton
978-1941070239

Demonology
Riley Star
978-19401070314

Pigeon Racing
Lolly Brown
978-1941070307

Dwarf Hamster
Lolly Brown
978-1941070390

Cryptozoology
Rex Cutty
978-1941070406

Eye Strain
Frederick Earlstein
978-1941070369

Inez The Miniature Elephant
Asher Ray
978-1941070353

Vampire Apocalypse
Rex Cutty
978-1941070321

Made in the USA
Las Vegas, NV
20 October 2020